The poems (... n, demonstrate close attentiveness to the natural world and express oneness with it: "let us lie down in the rain—/water inside, water outside." They are also rich and fluid, sensuous, awakening all the senses in landscapes we can see, hear, taste, touch, and smell. Taken together, they form a great love song to the Earth with its "cinnamon teals lifting/off the marsh," its "wind-scuffed glitter/along the tongue of the bay." These are necessary poems, born from an understanding of the need to protect our lovely blue-green planet, the only home we know.

–Lucille Lang Day,
author of *Becoming an Ancestor and Infinities*,
coeditor of *Fire and Rain: Ecopoetry of California*

Elizabeth Herron's poems in this collection seem to be written as pure love of the world of nature and her thorough assimilation of it, her immersion in it. Reading, you experience with her a merging into the greater whole of the other-than-human world, which for her is an embodiment of the sacred. "Before the mind awakes/the animal body remembers/the smell of salt and storms ... remembers itself/empty of language, empty of plans.... Then the mind rushes back ... and the animal body forgets its ever present small happiness. We rise/and step into words/and calendars and clocks/ and the long long grief."

–Gail Entrekin,
editor of *Canary* (canarylitmag.org),
author of *Rearrangement of the Invisible*

Like deep breaths drawn effortlessly in, the poems and images of *Insistent Grace* are satisfying to the core. Filled with the aromas of salt fog, summer grass, redwood creeks, eucalyptus, and bay, they weave together the human and the more-than-human worlds. It's a stunning intersection—buzzing with things I'd almost forgotten and others that were realized only on reading Elizabeth Herron's words. This is such a gift.

"We are always reinventing the world," she writes. The ripples from these poems carry that power—and reinvent the reader as well.

–Arthur Dawson,
poet, writer, editor and historical ecologist,
author of *Where the World Begins:
Sonoma Mountain Stories and Images*

Amazing grace, amazing poet! In the time of global pandemic and climate crisis, Elizabeth Herron evokes Mother Nature's insistent grace—a power that compels respect and can help us heal ourselves and our planet—if we are resolute.

–Marilou Awiakta,
author of *Selu: Seeking the Corn Mother's Wisdom*

Elizabeth Herron escapes the mundane, man-made world in favor of the feminine, natural one. Here time moves as slowly as the moon, as quickly as a pair of trout in a mating dance. Our senses say, "Yes, yes, I remember the scent of 'wood smoke and moldering leaves.'" The poet is our guide, leading us away from the overwhelming, specific present into an elemental time and space, where earth, sky, light, night, and creatures of all sizes invite us to join the dance. At a time when the natural world is so immediately threatened, Elizabeth Herron reminds us what it is we love so much about it.

Elizabeth is an alumna of the Mesa Refuge, a writing retreat where nature is the writer's constant companion. Days spent in silence there have done their work on her, so evident in her keen perception and lyrical phrasing.

–Susan Page Tillett,
executive director of Mesa Refuge

Insistent Grace

Elizabeth C. Herron

Fernwood
PRESS

Insistent Grace

https://elizabeth_herron.com
www.elizabethherron.net

Fernwood Press
Newberg, Oregon
www.fernwoodpress.com

Cover image: Deva Darshan
Cover and interior design: Mareesa Fawver Moss

Printed in the United States of America

ISBN 978-1-59498-070-1

for Brendan

Contents

I

II

III

Lake Trout

Those northern *salvelinus* mate
only on stormy autumn nights low
in the liquid layers like black glass

The male rubs the rocks clean
to lure the female in the glistening dark
and I dream of it, the white shaft
of lightning, a moon
and fast clouds, his
iridescent scales, the elegant
caudal fin she fans
as she waits, the way they
half-sink
together, instinct and ecstasy
in that cold place

below and apart
from the world of human desire
surfacing through sleep

Near the Woods

When the rain
lies down
in thick grass

When the wind
lies still
with the rain

What happens
at that meeting place?

Hush of—
and the animals
move through

Quiet

What is silence?
Something of the sky in us.
    —Ilya Kaminsky

It begins inside
and spreads
in concentric circles

A leaf drops
to the pond at dusk
ensnaring stars

Who Remembers

Here is the song of the neglected yellow moon.
—Jack Crimmins

Stones beneath the hawthorn,
rounded and whaled up
amid the sea of yellow leaves.

Who remembers the songs of stones,
the river that rolled them,
or the hawthorn, whose berries
healed hearts for generations?

Who remembers the songs
of pale alder, favorite of beaver,
yellow willow whose roots make baskets
fine enough to hold water,
or red-stemmed dogwood and wild currant
where sparrow, warbler and wren
flutter and feed?

Canada geese glide down
to winter pond at dusk, the marshy
muddy smell of home. Heart
by wing the geese know
where they belong

Listen deep. In the quiet
beyond thought—ancient stones,
creeks, rivers, roots, wings
and open branches
will sing you home.

Another World

After the guests have gone
the lights turned out

and wood heaped on the coals
the bright embers leaping to flame

wind outside and the trees
bowing to moonlight

Across the marsh a fox barks
and the dogs, foolish as city cops

on a dark country road
take up their alarms

knowing nothing
of the wiles of their cousins

or the ways of deer stepping from shadow
into the threaded fields

that stitch their lives from woods to creek
as the creek stitches the moon to the river

You there asleep in the east
I know you dream of this

waking to the *thunk* of another world
tossed to your door

Summer Weeds

At sunset we climb the hill
where I gather you
with the darkness
Your hair the rough fur
of some dream animal
your breath warm
as the earth
and all around us
the wild grass

so we go home
smelling of the summer
fields finding stickers
in our hair our clothes
to sleep turning
yarrow blossoms into stars
while barn owls sweep
the eaves above
our dreams

Like Longing

At home I am wild
in my privacy
eating avocado with lemon
and olive oil

naked in the garden
digging potatoes
my hands dark
with the damp earth

My skin smells of sun
and dry sweat
spicy
like a summer field flower

I brush my hair
and pale grass seeds fall
I keep all the doors
and windows open

the night invited
Desire is a green fruit
like longing but
not as blue

October Moon

That October moon
coming up like a collapsed pumpkin
Overripe as I—
October again
happy in spite of the lop-
sided way I climb
out of my bed

Fires of October

A living cell, like a flame, burns fuel . . . .
all these little fires spark the energy of life.
—Rachel Carson

I can imagine how each breath
takes in the light
and swirls it through
the billions of cells in my body

how each cell ignites with oxygen
in the chemical joy
of essential existence—
how it rises in the wings

of cinnamon teals lifting
off the marsh
to begin their migration—
how deep

in the icy waters of arctic lakes
the char glimmer
with the combustion of spawning
But what is it I must do

as the daylight narrows? Tell me
I whisper to the deepening dark
how to cradle that spark
to keep the fires of the mind
steadily burning ready

to open their fan of flame
the way the maple spreads
its crimson leaves across October
What ancient ritual song

am I meant to sing? Tell me
how to be the open hearth
the hollow waiting
to hold the mystery of this blaze

to be this radiance, even
to be ashes

Samhain

In the orchard
in the bright cold
of late October's angled light
the last windfall apples
cider into soil
seeking the damp
throat of earth
calling back
her summer songs

Autumn Song

The belly moon grows backward
to a sliver, then
the dark

The blossoms on the bough will wither
into the black bones of winter

Stark against the gray and empty sky
a hawk hangs high
above the field

And the sea rises
and the sea falls

Blood
passes through my body
from the other world

And the spirit rises
and the spirit falls

into winter's bare and open arms

And the sea rises
and the sea falls

into winter's bare and open arms.

Light's Descent

It was the downward movement of light that ignited the dust.
　　　—The Book of Angels

The last of Earth's face falls away
before the Moon of Long Snows

as the last longings lose their hold
when we near the brightness

of light alone, absent its cloak
of mud and blood

and the beautiful flesh—the leaves
the stones, the hidden brilliance

of sun behind clouds
above a winter horizon

tomatoes fallen to a smear of pulp and skin
summer's sweetness reduced

to the redolence of unpicked berries
caught in a collapsing bramble

The condensations of desire blur open
easing the light free, not to forget

the muck of matter surrendered and inert
dreaming its past life, but to burn

in the buzzard, the maggot, the mold
each darkness giving way in turn

to the memory of that first descent
with its surprise of wings

Animal Body

Before the mind awakes
the animal body remembers
the smell of salt and storms
wood smoke and moldering leaves
the muddy odor of marshes

Before the mind awakes
the animal body
turns in its familiar bed
in its own easy limbs
against the cotton quilt
under the open window
in the brush of dawn

Before the mind awakes
the animal body remembers itself
empty of language, empty of plans
and ideas, empty of daylight's surge
through shrouds of glass and asphalt

Before the mind awakes
the animal body still feels
its vanished companions

Then the mind rushes back
It remembers its missing objects
and the foolish mind
asleep on the night watch
startles into its defenses

It organizes the weapons
and calls forth the armies
and the animal body forgets
its ever-present small happiness
It no longer feels
the embrace of beauty

Thus the body's bereavement
is complete. We rise
and step into words
and calendars and clocks
and the long, long grief.

Moon Cradle

Caught in winter's sway
of branches, dark
smoothing the sky
to sleep, lullaby
of frog song
All these years
rummaging and still
this restless aching
toward

Lit Window

Willows along the creek bank
hunched against a faint salt haze
sucked in from the coast
and drawn up the valley
by twilight's chill
Rows of eucalyptus lining open fields
Someone walks past
the first lit window. Who is it
forgetting even the names of the dead
the quick hours
before starlight, forgetting
the tableware and teacups waiting
in another house
losing its walls in the dark?
Beneath the bent and blurring willows
with their muddy perfume, the water
let's itself go
to the Pacific, those willows
midwives at the streambed, backs bent
to the wind-whistled rim of the night

Three Nights of the Harvest Moon

for Eric and Jimalee

The first night I found my beloved
in the phosphorous glow of salt water—
an iridescence in the splash of an oar
under the full moon through fog
so thick across the bay
we couldn't see the island from the land

You can't save time, my beloved said
You can only spend it
Rich or poor, better or worse
it runs through your fingers
faster than gold, my beloved told me

The *dynoflagellates* are smaller
than grains of sand, I said
and rarely visible. It takes this oar
to turn their bodies into light
And as for time—what is its velocity?
The speed of love is all that can outrun it

The second night I found my beloved
in a four-point buck
caught in the headlights as he struggled
in the ditch by the side of the road—
the lift of his crowned head held level

through the white light and his blurred
confusion of nerve and muscle
unresponsive to the sheer drive
of his heart to rise from the earth
his legs buckled under him

We turned back, left the car
its engine silenced
in the windless night
to sit beside the buck
who had fallen farther then
toward the hum of his own darkness

lying long-wise in the ditch
when the spasm of death
shuddered through him
Eric tucked his straightened legs back under
and we stroked his coat awhile
feeling the stillness deepen

Faster than gold through your fingers
my beloved escaped with a sigh
into the breath of fog
that touched my hair, my face, the grass
and rocks of the rough field.

The third night I found my beloved
in the resonance of the monastery bell
just past twilight
before the moon rose
and he stayed with me
till my tumbling thoughts hushed
and I received him and found him

everywhere—
crickets rubbing their legs
over the warm starlight
the path of fiery fallen leaves
lit by the porch lamp

that moon rising and rising
through the redwoods

where I waited while time slid away
faster than gold
till the moon was high and distant
and a cold wind came in
across the quiet mountain.

Initiation

Enter the land between certainties
Repeat the spell of renunciation

Through the trees the words fly
loose like your hair, the air
laced with them. The bay laurel

bunched on the hills
roll toward you like sheep
in a storm—you feel dizzy

when their oily scent
shoves up the canyon
Near the creek
you find the right rock

and lean your head
against its granite flank
The water ripples
with the rush of song

from the willows
the dogwood, the wild azalea
the stutter of leafless alders
against the colorless sky—

where all the blue, all the gray
has settled in your heart
pressing you down

down
    down

through leaves, through topsoil
through the *mychorrizal* web
with its thousand thin white fingers
You descend

through earth into bedrock
through layers of time
pressed between crystals
into the molten core
of the most ancient

Reduced to pattern
as the star is in the flower
as the flower is in the seed
you do not know
who you are

When you return you will meet
all that remains of you. Only then
will you know what you have become.

II

Hearthkeeping

Breathing embers into flame
at the hearth at midnight, the clothes
tangled and tumbling in the dryer
Calm spreads in me
as I prod the logs
into their alchemy and listen

as the coyotes' overlapping howls
rise to a sharp crescendo
then descend
to rise again, summersaulting
down the valley

The quickened fire snaps
pine-pitch hot and nearly white, a nest
of wings from the underside, blue
in the bed of night

The coyotes move north under cold stars
Only the fire speaks, the dryer stopped
though heaven and earth keep turning,
and the clothes hold the heat
of their spin-spin-spinning

Winter's Stone

The heart falters
then grows calm
solitary wren
in the bare bramble
Cooper's Hawk
close under trees

Blue Cup

All night the wind raged
between the trees and house. Even now
it stutters against the shingles, thrashes
the branches—a fist shaking the sky

Yesterday's laundry, abandoned on the line
leaps and snaps with such ferocity it seems
the towels will shred into wings and fly
Last stars a windswept grit
in the deep blue dawn beyond the window

I've coaxed the coals of last night's fire to embers
and blown a small blaze. Hands warmed
around a mug of tea, I step outside
into the blue cup of the world
finding the moon
a bright hard slice in the indigo east
fast fading into light, the marsh
a glaze of pewter
and a horizon rimmed rose

Out here in the wind-scudded trees
I can see exactly how far south
this darkest of all nights took the sun
behind which tree it will rise
this dawn when the sun tolls
the burnished bowl of the heart
    return return return

Winter Storm

From winter sky a spool of rain
threads the valleys with silver
to the sea

where you parted and broke
the narrow strips of light
disturbing the beauty

of its refracted web
It wove you back—
your wounds your life returned

to prismatic relations. There
in the water, the hard light
at the center of the world

softens receptive as fire
but gentle, more forgiving
All the clutter and litter of multiplicity

spun back to source
to be woven again till of a piece
we share that enviable indifference

And we shall be the stippled creeks
the moon both whole and broken
the stuttering fire the wet wood

the roots intertwined
and stitched into earth
the very slips of light

that break and mend
in this fallen and gathered
this lost and found
this fierce insistent grace

Rain

My friend, let us lie down in the rain—
water inside, water outside
Tell me again how it was
when the salmon came up the rivers
what rivers were they?

The Eel, the Russian, the Navarro, Big River,
the Gualala, the Madd—all the rivers
You'd see these vees the shape of an arrow
moving upstream because it ran off their dorsal fins
and left a wake widening behind them

And was there a vee for each fish?

Each one made a vee. You'd see several vees together
and you'd know it was the salmon

What salmon were they? What were their names?

Steelhead, coho, king—*mykiss, kisutch, tshawytscha*

I've heard older stories—how the river
was a single roiling thing, thick with them
from bank to bank, thousands
surging home

We love the rain. It remembers

our fishness. How once we were water
how we'd make a vee

We stand under the overhang
looking out at the storm
swinging down from the Gulf of Alaska—
two fish, underwater swimming upstream
in the rain, maybe like this

When we thrash over the riffle
our dorsal fins exposed
rain wet, river wet, we are
fish, river, water
swimming the world
into its birth salt sea, remembering

February

When everything I've fought for
falls away
bright wind
leafless branches
rock the winter moon

Winter Morning

The red bark maple's delta splay
of branches—

Frost in icy currents following the grain
of the picnic table—

The garden giving way to sun—

Railing spindles that shadow
the wide deck planks
caging the slatted light—

One quick slap of her paw
to break the ice in her bowl
and the dog drinks

I love this shape-shifter world—
the frost and its fading
riverine winter trees
shadows
breaking need and the joy of thirst
giving way to cold water

Silk/Light

Beads of dew no bigger than the center hole
of a button where the thread goes through
strung along filaments of spider's silk, hung
in a complex cat's cradle
between the sprigs of coyote bush

against the gray-white morning sun
so diffused through fog the sky
is a single radiance of damp translucent air
The spare outer strands thicken and jumble
toward center in a pattern too fine

for the naked eye, dense
as a crowded nebula, bodies of light
bound by gravity and proximity—a dendrite
exploding light
in the inner space of the body, spinning

and spinning—this web. The hidden silk
of caddis larvae, spun inside scratchy cases
of leaves and bark and grains of river gravel
holding those bits together, and holding
with the silken stitch they've made

to rocks under riffled water, a silken net
at the crusts open end to filter plankton in
These holy insect houses, essential
and entrained in the woven world—these
delicate miracles, these hallelujahs!

Mid-March Spawners

At the end of the deer trail down to the water
under the three alders that fell last winter
in a pool on the far side of the gravel bar—
a density of shadow, a steelhead salmon

in and out of shallows. He skates fast over gravel
twists sideways—a scimitar half in air
sleek and limber, he darts back to sidle up
beside the hen holding at the top of the pool

He threads her like a needle, over and back, over
and back, as if he could stitch himself to her
Camouflaged with dappled light, speckled and smooth
she's hidden till she turns and whips her body

so she shines like a polished pan
under the water, shakes herself, unfurling
silver light that makes the gravel, roots and
drifting saffron bay leaves pale

The buck shudders beside her
swings away, loops out over the gravel bar
to a patch of sun, glistening
dorsal fin straight up, he gapes. He's flying
curved clean out of water, chasing off a young jack
that darts in and hangs around in the riffle
waiting to steal the hen. He's lithe and quick

not more than six or seven inches, golden
without the sea-run gun-barrel blue of the buck

The hen stays put, hidden again, till she tilts
gleams and quivers, undulating fast
all light gathered to her, then
rights herself, uses her tail to work the gravel

I follow the jack upstream, stop back later
The buck is all I see, drifting down. Then
hopping the cobble, he twists, shoots the riffle
skitters up the shallows to the pool, like a lover
going back to smell the sheets

Ear

The small bones
and cartilage
the timpanic membrane
and the delicate hairs
whose cells catch waves
of sound and pass them
to the auditory nerve
of the brain that decodes
the tonal frequencies
and contours of progression—
the more I hear hallelujah
everywhere
a place for praise

Rustler

A day the sun haloed sheep
against gray winter fields
Trails crisscrossing
the hills and fences
what they know of home

they turned backs to the wind
that northern rustler
who kept me company, driving
the flocked clouds south

I was headed for the open
road and a dangerous
nostalgia filled me, knowing
where this world takes us
is far away, past sleep

Dead Snake

Ovoviporous snakes hatch their eggs inside
and bear their young live. But she was hit
torn open by the tire, and here they are
half out her, some dragged and blurred
over the pavement. Close to term, perfect

tiny replicas of her—gray-brown, the long
stripe down her side pale green or yellow gold
It's hard to tell with the dust and the way
the color fades when life goes. What if
they were inside me, so if you slit me open

they would spill out in a slithering lump?
Think of my own eggs in their thin sacks
like the granular roe of shad pressed
to the roof of my mouth with my tongue
or translucent, glistening like flying fish roe

which I eat on sticky white rice. My eggs
a delicacy wasted, one by one
in their lonely descent, their brief lodging
their final exit beautifully wrapped
in their bloody bedding. I wish you could see

how deep and red it is, how it flowers
open on white cotton, or blossoms
on water, widens, fades into a pale pink
tinge. Sometimes so thick even clotted
the drops hold their shape the way fudge

after you've beaten it a long time
holds together when you drop it into cold
water off the end of a spoon—this
rich blood, this necessary nourishment
my body gives up, belongs to the Mother's garden

as this snake, medusa bellied, unarticulated
eye still clear and shining, this sad and beautiful
snake, swinging grotesque
and miraculous in her holy multiplicity
when I lift and carry her on a stick

to the grass beside of the road—already
she is everywhere, her eggs the still green
beaded buds amid the small sharp leaves
of coyote bush will open creamy white
flowers staining the hills
with the smell of honey

Psalms

It might have been the wind
The light billowed

through the room
Leaves swept the wall in shadow-sails

The steady snarl of the neighbor's mower
passing cars, and the distant thrum

of the water treatment pumps
fell silent behind the bright gusts

The strangling apex of summer
loosened and released its heat

The blossoms of poor-man's orchid
snapped and spit their seeds

the fists of blackberries softened
and grew dark

the proud grasses collapsed
against the dust, and the Mexican primroses

reached a spindly height
sighed and withered, petals creased

as a grandmother's cheek
I entered the narrow place

of my own life, and it reeled open
with the wind that wheeled through the room

to seize the tight words of my thoughts
and my knotted heart and surge

into the trees and spiral to swift clouds
hinged on the nuances of light

and wordless whispered psalms
as the wind leapt past

Rooster

He's outwitted wild dogs
survived single-minded cyclists
roosted in ratty willows above a bramble
pecked grubs and crumbs
and now he races toward me
not scolding but some reproach –
how could I
come with only a dime
in my pocket
useless as last night's moon
no chicken scratch
or crust? He gives me
one golden eye in its target of white
feathers and waits
while I apologize
for not having thought of him once
after all he's gone through
to stay alive.

Breaking Drought

Humps of coyote bush herded
beside the path
to the gate. Dandelions
dotting the drowsy garden

Confetti of chive
arugula and onion petals
like torn bits of daytime-moon
afloat their stems

A sky quilted with we-wish-rain

Empty rope-swing

Blue jays scratchy talk

A dog barking down the hill

The cat swings his tail and sniffs
for what came by in the night

This world does what it does
if I am here or not

Now a spatter of drops
like the faint irregular ticking
of the sky's own clock

As Light Escapes

Bent to the house of leaves and string
I forage for peas in the garden

split the chrysalis cradles
with a thumb—green pearls

in my palm. I eat them raw—sun
on my back, then go in

and fold into the wicker chair
On the wall, the Chinese painting—

bare branches, blue-gray sky
Vees of white birds lifting up

Like that, I think
we will leave our dark husks

as light escapes a closed room
when you open the door

Rue

Unpinning a sheet from the line
I press my face to the clean smell of sun
the sheet huge for my queen bed
and white as a bandage

This morning for my slim hope
I soaked the flowerpot
with the dwarf orchid
that hasn't bloomed in years

afterward watching the water
spin down the drain
I thought of Aleppo
    (wells bombed
      aid convoys blown up
      before they unload)

The orchid's green roots glistened
wet. My hands curved around the pot
the way they might around the seed
of a fetus. I'd tell it

to go back, tell it the world
is not a safe place now
    (bloody
      and covered with dust)

Impossible Grace

At the edge of the bay
the great blue heron
raised one branched foot
to lift and place it down again
on the slick back
of the marsh
The other foot followed
and in this way the heron walked
toward the bank
The clouds shifted
and he was doubled
on the water's sun-gilt surface
before he disappeared in the sedge
leaving me blessed
as a guest in Galilee
honey on my lips instead of wine
I followed the dark clouds home
weightless riding
the heron's wide gray wings
and when the hallelujah moon
rose through the redwoods
I knew the song
of her broken light

Ritual

for Lewis Hyde

To make a fertile body
shave this stone
with a pen knife

carefully round
Make a paste
to smooth across

your thighs, breasts
the hard bones
of your back

Baby tears will grow
all over you, a second
skin, a vegetable fur

a thousand green faces
smaller than your
baby fingernail. You

will be their ground
When you write
remember the blank page

like the bones of the year's first
salmon, thrown back
to the water

by which the spirit
returns
to the sea

Imagine It

Imagine it—the space where that split
does not exist, dark and half-forgotten
A wide river, fields of wild grass
You know the worst stories—
the terror and grief
ancient as the sword and the clock
Now's your chance—earth, body, womb, night—
imagine it. We are always
reinventing the world
Begin where you are: light
through liquid amber leaves
silver-gray grasses
lying down toward winter
draped along the bed of the dry marsh
waiting for rain. Begin now
with me. All this light—
more than the eye or the mind or the heart
can take. Do you see
how our skin melts into it?
Whatever darkness holds the seed
is always moving, opening to light, petals
becoming formless sky. Imagine it—
a seed like a closed fist opening
Your life like that
no matter how you hold what you hold.

The Mind's Light

There is the sun
and the wayward light
of the moon
and the light of the mind

that sometimes goes dark

The homeless vet
who mutters and curses
by the ATM
curls in the doorway now
dreaming again
he holds the child telling her
Don't look back don't look back

His bed tonight
is cardboard on concrete. Asleep
he sees her lit face
who might in the way of dreams

be more than herself—his soul
rests on this repeated rescue
no one else can see

Who is to say where light resides?

Dust of Life*

Bui doi they call the half-American
children of Vietnamese women.
I learned this
the day I heard
a baby was found alive
in a trash compactor
the same day
a homeless man died
when the dumpster he was sleeping in
was picked up by the truck.
Dumpsters are warm
because decomposition is an active process.
That might be what kept the baby
alive. The homeless man slept
perhaps like a baby.
I lie awake
rummaging the dust and refuse
of my mind offering up what it can.
Tonight I forgive myself
for not being able to spin straw to gold
or make shoes
or sing a baby to sleep

Bui doi translates from Vietnamese to "dust of life."

Fawn on Bodega Highway

Her head lolls when I lift her

legs a spindly sway
below the roil of translucent intestine

No odor of death
only the scent of her mother's milk

Take her to the dandelions and vetch
the foxglove with their spotted throats
under the thyrse blossoms of buckeye

The doe browses alone now

crosses the meadow in the morning uneasy
sense of nothing behind her

the hollow open where light had gathered
into form and slid bloody in a sack of pearl
to the grass beside her

Still astonished she turns
listening

hesitates

suspended in the throb of her flanks
the curdle of her grassy milk.

Animal

On the hump of rock
between the little gulches that drop off
either side where the scat collects
I sit and look at it, pleased
to find this evidence of animal

I look over the lake—
animal eyes what would you see?
Listen to the wind—
animal ears what would you hear?

I break open your scat
to see what you eat, finding only
the alfalfa odor of baling and barns
No bones, no small claw, tiny tooth
or mat of fur, no seed or pit
as in the bear scat south of here
along the Tuolumne

You will find your scent released afresh
from my search for your name—
marmot. You give me comfort
in the solitude that scours me bare

At night I nudge the logs into last heat
and undress by the fire
For a moment I am something else
in the quivering light
with eyes and ears and teeth
of my own.

Wild Blackberries

I'm prepared to get in deep
to find the ripest berries, picking
the patch across the back of the hill
where nothing else grows but thistles
their down billowed between dry stalks

Father and son are having their talk
on the porch of the house below
while high to the west
the carpenters work
shirtless in the heat
setting rafters on the new house
that will breathe down our necks
young and raw pitched there

The carpenters balance aloft
like Michelangelo's angels
on lusty 2 x 12s, their torsos glossy
with sweat, their voices
drifting down as father and son's
float up, all the words simmering
in the heat of mid-day

Each berry a constellation
of dark drops holding a tiny star
every berry a sweet swarm, and I'm reaching
heedless of thorns.

Vanishing

Heart, lungs and gut gone to the gnaw
of insects, the intact hull of her
beached on redwood duff, prickly
oak and pine needles, coyote scat
in the crook of her knee

Trellie sniffs the small sharp hoof
ignoring the heap of dung,
red with the berries of madrone,
pale pits pearling through. She noses
the foreleg where scraps of hide
still cling to bone.

I imagine the first flick of tail, ripple of skin
under summer flies—how
did this fawn die?

The woods are full of stories
in rotting trunks, cool shadows and bones
like these whitened by winters
the fawn would never see

But what of her stays with me? Days later
in my old green chair by the window
cat on the ottoman
and curved around my feet
Trellie denned under the table,
cup on the sill, I remember

the coyote—its blond and bloated body
on the road, a plastic bag hoof-snagged
ballooning beside a patch of dry
blood-slicked fur.

Will the silence of their absence rise
above the din of cities? Will their ghosts
stumble through strip malls and suburbs
looking for lost meadows,
jostle at the on-ramps, distracting drivers
with a sudden vague unease?

Will our grief surprise us?
Will we wonder at our loneliness?

The Stones, the Dark Earth

Pell-mell into daylight
carried forth toward spring
through the sleighs of winter
wandering from post to post
carried toward light
through the dim branches
the hidden hollows of ice
the gold gleam of sun
through frozen limbs
We cannot remember before
the amber dark hummed with honey
We were wild with it
mouth to mouth dreaming
sweet liquid, our longing
neither there nor here
but in the very healed and holy
dreams we gave each other
For this always
is the way the turning moves—
richness too deep, the dark hold
a womb of stars
breath of sorrow
brought beside the joy

For every union speaks of separation
every gain of loss
rhythmic as breathing, as seasons

There will be that—
when those around us let us go
disinterested finally
in our slow exploration of stones
our simple turning
toward winter sunlight
And left to ourselves we savor
the random sounds of distant voices
the puzzle of hours
that order and re-order themselves
in a shiftless history
So a life is lived many times
until the last husk
discarded as an old carapace
a split chrysalis
or skin left to dust
So each holy creature—hummingbird
golden-frog ant worm flotsam of plankton—
each miracle is embraced
and abandoned
each longing leading toward

Returning

We enter the woods
like walking in
to water, slowly
we submerge

The head floats off—
each cell with its own brain
Now we see with our skin

All around us the deer—
their ears like candles
flickering with each sound

Above us the tall trees creak
like the rigging
of ancient ships
and owls shake off
the feathers of their sleep

Remembering

Where are your women?*

If you were the father of perfect formulas, perfect passwords
to underground shelters, to the tops
of skyscrapers, the flawless carpet and the wide glass window

If you were the father of Progress, the father of Hurry, father
of the hijacked dream, father of the snapshot
of the woman no one ever met

Father—
I would ask you

if you remembered
how the flame celebrates itself—the log, the air
the veil of smoke rising
how the embers fly up toward the stars
when the logs crumble

as surely as the summer garden after first frost
the dark cave-ins when light escapes. How beautiful
the blurred ink, the blood cycle
of the world giving way to itself

*What the Cherokee asked when the white men came to talk.

III

Mother Time

Time cool as a melon
under a sharp knife

The moon coming up
with slurred slowness

A summersault of hours
downhill, rocking
a lullaby though I sleep
fitfully, dreaming
a blurred roulette
of bicycle wheels
a future spinning
into autumn apples
falling to damp gold grass
the last blackberries
on the tangled barbed-
wire bramble

Sun
perfect as pie
through the south window

The fir tree in stiff silhouette

Inside this
whole and needless stillness
change begins
its erotic bloom

Conspiracy

Summer moon. Inside
avalanche. Touch
like prayer

The Wheel of It

As if the mist were a path
in a swelling birth of mind

I pass wind-bent willow in the gullies
coyote bush in rock-strewn fields

over the curving hills
beside the wind-scuffed glitter

along the tongue of the bay
through the bright air

across the creek with its lean
limbs all sway

in their reach to the sea
Read the land's secret script

Swing, it says, swirl swerve
sweep spin sail branch bend bow—

the wheel of it
the twist and snake of it

the tug of swift certainty
sure as a voice or a light

in the rounding way back home

Annie's Field

Annie's field is empty now
She foundered after eating green
lay in the rain till dawn
neighbors noticed she was down

I might see her dapple-gray ghost
in the sprawl of mist and moonlight
if I should stop
at the rusty tangled barbed-wire
where she stood
on the beaten-bare ground

season after season
flies buzzing at her milky eye
in summer, in rain and winter frost
frozen on her coat and mane
matted with mud

She might canter toward the trees
as she was
before she lost the luster hope brings
If you can love something
for what it was, I do

but I keep walking
up the darkened lane
to throw my hand with the living—
gamblers

who pitch their hearts to chance
hard-drinking men at the bar
the tomcat yowling from the yard
disgraced as any lover in his ache

I keep walking
past the blind light of the neighbor's barn
past where the wren has fled
from the safe shadows of her nest
past the memory of Annie
waiting by the fence

You can love something for what it was
and for the blue patience
made of loneliness

Faye Creek

The perfect tracks of doe and fawn
follow the bank
under the overhang of green
where the creek ripples
with weightless water-skates
in a broidery of light
on stones and water raddled
with reflections—the doe's print

larger with a slight splay, the fawn's
delicate points where the tips meet
Crouched over the tracks
I think of the fawn I found on the road
still warm, her limp neck no bigger
than my forearm

I think of Wolfgang Laib
gathering pollen, sifting it through linen
into heaps of gold. Bees and honey
the months the fawn grew—
a condensation of light
in a watery world of breath and heartbeat

Here by the creek the world receives itself—
leaf and stone, lichen and branch
catkin and alder cone
Steelhead fry flick past half-disguised

by bay leaves mirrored on the water
or soggy and dark on the gravel bottom

What silence, what tender listening
caught the fawn with her last breath
gently as pollen
collected from a blossom?

To Be Called

In fall foliage
the spangled lantern
of Japanese maple
lights the morning garden
The hawthorn's red berries
sun-struck, glisten
Last night the gibbous moon
ignited frost on the trash can lids
Day or night
reverence rises from the ordinary
To hold the moment, wanting nothing
is to behold eternal presence only
waiting recognition. The quiet heart
receives. The ungrasping eye sees
how the world longs to give itself
how underneath all longing
we long to be called
to praise

Borrowing

So each man must yield the lease-hold of his days.
    —Beowulf

What after all do we own in this life?
The moon through shuddering oaks
borrows its light
Wouldn't it be better if from the start
we knew the truth—
that only our souls belong to us
and they too only
for the lease-hold of our days
and little we know that number
or what comes after?
Astonishing in sunlight the lilies
have split their long buds to open
each separate petal
ignited like the moon
as if from within
Remember spring's first grass?
That same impossible incandescence
we once held and now
must bring from within
to burnish and share
without apparent purpose. Light
escaping everywhere—in the bodhisattva
who passes no judgment, the bum
asleep on the bus, the girl walking alone

on her way to school, or the man
in Tiananmen Square, side-stepping
to stay in the path of the tank. Light—
the flood of it! Brief and unforgettable
The lilies, the broken moon

Year After Year

Solitude
and autumn's letting go
a bleak winter courage
trust in spring
summer's ripe fields
till at last
I become the harvest
and the scythe
cuts me down

Migration

If my words can be
as honest as desire
they will go to you
like a flow of caribou over ice
they will lick the air
like a migration of wild geese spill
like salmon upstream
words of a primal instinct
pulling you
into an urgent journey knowing
though you know not where
you're going home

Might Be

This morning might be the beginning
of the world might be the beginning
of an eon an era—this sun
that kettle humming from the stove
might be the beginning—a stone
a seed a whistle a whisper beginning

Humming from the stove might be
a beginning—a whisper a whistle a rap
on the mind's back door

The mind's back door might be a trap
door down
to the cellar with all its might-be-
baskets of apples and onions and walnuts
shelves of canned peaches and tomatoes
Might be down there plenty
to eat

Baskets and jars on the shelves to eat
might be dreaming of summer—
might be longing for sunlight longing
to go back into earth
might be longing for earth

Sunlight longing for summer longing for earth
might be the beginning
might be the spool

of darkness down
in the cellar in the baskets

spooled with summer might be darkness
might be baskets might be the silence
of summer

waiting to begin again an era of sunlight
a world of leaves and humming might be
blossoms or seeds might be the beginning
in the back of the mind might be a rapping
might be a whisper might be

Might be a whisper a whistle a kettle
Might be a moon a basket a beginning

Might be a doorway—a doorway
might be an arrival might be an opening
might be a beginning—

a whisper a whistle a trap-
door down. Might be a morning sun
through leaves might be
a humming

A humming might be the beginning
might be earth or sunlight
might be the baskets the plenty to eat
might be eating
an era of endings might be seeds spit back
Might be the moon coming and going dark
and light—God

eating
plenty of moons
over eons. Might be eons.

Today might be the beginning might be God
spitting back plenty to eat

Seeds might be the moon—a whisper
a whistle a basket a nest an ear might be
listening
Might be a basket
a doorway a whisper a whistle
Might be a wing
Might be a seed
Might be a beginning might be
a song

Acknowledgments

Thank you to the editors of the following journals, where some of these poems first appeared, sometimes in alternate versions:

> *Reflections*, "To Be Called" & "Who Remembers"
> *Oberon Magazine*, "Light's Descent" (*Oberon* Annual
>   Poetry Award, Honorable Mention)
> *The Wayfarer*, "The Wheel of It" & "Fires of October"
> *West Marin Review*, "As Light Escapes"
> *Free State Review*, "Dead Snake"
> *Lindenwood Review*, "Fawn on Bodega Highway"
> *Critical Pass Review*, "Lit Window"
> *Eco-Citizen*, "Meanwhile Music"
> *Chagrin River Review & Anthology of Chagrin River
>   Poets*, "Instructions" & "Dust of Life"
> *Canary*, "Vanishing" (nominated for a Pushcart Prize
>   in Poetry, 2020)

Earlier versions of the following poems appeared first in *The Stones, the Dark Earth*, a chapbook from Harlequin Ink, Falmouth, MA:

"Silk/Light"

"Impossible Grace"

"Three Nights of the Harvest Moon"

"Imagine It"

"Hearthkeeping"

"The Stones, the Dark Earth"

"Lake Trout"

Of the many friends who have supported my work, I want to thank especially Kim Clement and Ardath Lee for always asking, being willing to read, and responding with honesty and enthusiasm to my poems. Thanks to Jack Crimmins for hours over years of sharing our writing, and for his endless willingness to read my latest and talk process. Jan Beaulyn, Patricia Damery, Jimalee Plank and Norma Churchill have long listened and made good suggestions, but more than this, they have been steadfast friends. Gratitude always to Mike Traynor for years of friendship, good advice and the inspiration to do my best. None of my present life would have been possible without him. Thanks to Francisco Vasquez for his trust and friendship; they came at the perfect time. For her wisdom, love and all the times we laughed together, I am forever grateful to Frances Vaughan. Lastly, for his patience, encouragement, and outrageous imagination, fathomless gratitude goes to Brendan Smith, my partner in art and love.